Geoff Goodfellow

First published 1986
Reprinted 1986, 1988,
1989 (twice), 1990, 1991.

Front cover designed by Liane Thomas.

First published by Friendly Street Poets.

Published in 1992 by Wakefield Press,
43 Wakefield Street, Kent Town, South Australia, 5067.

Printed by Federal Printing House Pty. Ltd.
20 O'Brien Street, Adelaide, South Australia, 5000.

National Library of Australia card number
and ISBN 0 949363 07 3

for my three sons
Mark, Shane and Paul

Acknowledgements

Ash
The Australian Literary Magazine
Big Bang
Contact
Crow Magnus
Fremantle Arts Review
Friendly Street Poetry Readers 8, 9
Germinal
Independent Teacher
Larrikin
Meanjin
Mattoid
Nunga News
Overland
Patterns
"R"
Turnstyle
Undercurrent
Vision
Words And Visions

5CL
5MMM
3CR

Poems

Locked In

Beware of The Penguins

the first school for me
   was one that made young
boys   into little men
   (till grade four)
& young girls
   into little ladies
with straw hats

school was uplifting for me
with Sister Mary what's-her-name
   lifting me off the boards
by my left ear   arms
   flailing like a windmill

& she did

until that parent/teacher day
   in the quadrangle
& i said
     do it now
     do it now

i often remember
that protesting penguin
with the red face   & it wasn't
hot flushes that day

in summer   classes
under the gums singing
multiplication songs
   even fourteen times
tables   & i still sing them
   but now
on the bathroom scales
   where everything is changing

sitting at that flip
top desk   eastern side
of the class for the morning sun
   in prickly grey melange

she'd eyeball me

3

then beat that short
thick heavy leather strap
into her palm & tell me
    don't write left handed
OR ELSE!
    sick people silly people
crazy people in hospitals
write left handed!

& i worried

& changed

then beat allcomers in the
left handed arm wrestles
    & i worried
if i could still go crazy

& i saw the girl
who sucked her thumb
in grade three
    crawl around the classroom
on all fours
    dummy in mouth

& i saw the girl
who dribbled regularly
on her desk top   get her nose
rubbed in it
    & i can still see
snail trails
    shining off her desk top
on my way to recess

a sixpenny cream bun
    icing sugar
smothering my freckles
    dandruff
down my Silver Fleece Jumper

& i still love
strawberry jam

but when i go to the zoo
now
    i usually give
the penguins
    a miss.

Lost Gold

we grew up in a street
full of post-war kids
   3 brothers
bunk bedded as the rest
   evenly spread
with grey army blankets
   blue striped
to match our eyes

through summer holidays
we'd strip to shorts
   the beds to sheets
then canopy
the clothes-hoist grey
   & spruik the street
for starters

with towels for gloves
we drove our noses flat
   fat-lipped
we had our dreams
   & when the blankets
grew too thin
   our hides not thick
enough
   we found old Max

singing to a skipping rope
that hummed in tune
   he moved   supple
as the leather gloves
& punching bags that hung
with tin-shed sweat
& yellowed posters

& the youngest
   stayed the longest

turned his dream into
a crown

together
   we saw Olympic Trials
vanish through double glazed
hospital windows
   on a Shylock bite of thigh
from a circular saw

5

while dreams were nursed
& main events remembered
    he punched out one-liners
like
a bloody shark got me mate

& the trophies
    that dulled to blanket grey
to the colour of that
saw blade
    now catch the flash
of blue eyes
    when he passes.

The Gift

i sometimes smile
passing that bus shelter
in Galway Avenue
    thinking back
to that Xmas of 1960
& the morning me & Pete
sharpened the axe
on dad's oval grindstone
    the ¼" BLACK & DECKER
revving its guts out
    sparks flying in all directions

we filled mum's shiny preserving pan
    put it on the gas stove
went out the back
    dressed for the kill

24 bloody chickens
cartwheeled around the yard
looking for their heads
    while we sat red-flecked
on spears of buffalo grass

watching life pump away

eating warm apricots
& talking about what we would've
done to those bloody Nips
if we'd been up there
in the islands a generation back

& on the boil
    we untied their legs
from the rotary clothes line
    drove our tight fists
into the unknown
    drew back   flicked out
over old newspapers
& dunked into mum's big pan
    & the steamy stench
of plucked feathers
    sure didn't smell
like mum's stewed apricots

& while we cleaned up
     wound a shoe box
with yards of intestines
livers & hearts
     pinched some of mum's
Xmas wrapping & a card
& wrote
          To Dear Helen
          hope you have a Merry Xmas,
          Love,
               Nana.

& left it
     on the bus shelter seat

i sometimes smile
     passing that bus shelter
in Galway Avenue
     thinking back
to that Xmas of 1960
& crisp chicken skin
     the succulence of wings
& parsons noses
     & what a bastard of a kid
i was.

The Apprenticeship

out of school at 15
   under-educated by
2 Techs were gingham
& melange never touched
   & even conversation
was out-of-bounds
   i jerked the handle
of a sausage filler
for 5 quid a week
   argued over an hour's
overtime each paynight

scored 10 or so victories
by a short half head
when the boss said
   you're too up-front
to be out-back   wear a tie
on Monday

& it was mirrors
   laminex
   stainless steel
& old reflections

the polished floor
   covered with sawdust
like Friday night dancehalls
where girls grew crimson
in a Moon River embrace
   & left me
to untangle my tongue
& talk to the boys

& back at the counter
   i was as blank as
butcher's paper
   contending with ladies
more up-front than my
imagination
   as i stumbled speechless
over sawdust

but serving in that
butcher's shop
i learnt to talk to women
   & realize now

the need for balanced diet.

Ghosts

i know 35 pints
on a Saturday
 is excessive

i know .26
 is too high

& i know
 when there's a warrant
out for a mirror image
 & you think
you're a ghost
 you're a clown

ghosts
 don't wear tattoos
ghosts don't display
Homeward Bound
on their right bicep
 don't grow beards
drive trucks
or carry union cards
& ghosts are never there
 when they're wanted

well
 you're not a ghost now
you're a statistic
 & an empty chair at home
for Xmas dinner
 but i s'pose you'll have
cold turkey long before then

i know
 you can roll your own
& you can do it standing
on your head
 but grey cotton twill
doesn't do you justice

& homeward bound
 you're not.

Amnesia

8.00 a.m. & the door's
rattling in its frame
    get in   i says
jeez   *y' look like*
death warmed up

well i've had a win
but then got pipped
on the post
    spent a day running
from the beer garden
to the TAB
    got out of it
in the last
    $100 on the nose
at 4/1   *but then i've got*
into the Pernod   *doubles*

dunno what's happened
but this copper's woke me up
at 4 o'clock
    number One Angas Street-
wants me prints
    well i've bunged on
a nice blue   *thought*
i was home & i'm tellin' him to
    empty himself
he's finished up snarling

i dunno what you've done
i've just gotta get y'r prints

& they've let me out
on this blue form
    $100 bail on me own
recognizance
    but i dunno what i've done
bark off me elbows
    lump on me scone
got me beat

the defacto sister-in-law
hits him with black coffee &
    didn't you know
double Pernods cause amnesia

i've broken the blankness with
well   i'll jump on the
eau-de-cologne & give 'em
a blast if y' want

go fer it he says
   i'd love to know

the voice comes through
as blunt as a pencil
   Watch-house Sergeant

look   me brother's
just lobbed home with a bail
form   what's he been
charged with?

he should've asked
before he left   name

Goodfellow

sounds like he's been a
badfellow to me

so i says
   keep y'r day job   that one
was worn out by schoolteachers
20 years ago

hmmm   disorderly behaviour
resisting arrest

so i took up the slack
in me line & pulled him in with
   s o u n d s   l i k e   p o l i c e
h a r a s s m e n t   t o   m e

he's jumped in like a main eventer
why don't y' lodge a complaint —
get in touch with y'r local MP

well   i tried that
a few years back
   me mouthpiece told me to drop off
'cos y' can't beat a uniform
   they'll square up the next week
around the corner

12

yeah   spot on
     so why don't y' tell y'r brother
to stop drinking & stay at home
     i don't go out like that meself

& i says yeah   well no-one
would ASK YOU   would they
clunk
     beep
          beep
               beep
                    beep
                         beep...

Mum's The Word

all the men are boys
to her   now all the
boys are men
    & mum's the word

& in that serviceman's house
    twenty one bus stops
& four pubs from town
    the old boy   he's drilled 'em
y' don't break the code
    like   mum's the word
till it rings in ears
like a primal chant

& mum's the word when
trouble breaks   a nose
    an eyebrow   the early
morning call
assault police we've locked
him up will you come down

& mum's the word when
colours change   i've seen
her go through pastel pink
    crimson red   ghostly grey
when yellow turns to green
    & bells begin to ring

& all her men are boys
    still playing games with
odds so short they'll never win
    gamblers
all with different games to play
    & when their number's up
hers is on
    & mum's the word.

The Days Of My Mother

Mum
    according to the official
Australian life tables
relating to womens'
life expectancy
    at 64 years of age
not allowing for leap years
to complicate my equations

we can look forward to
    hearing your laughter
    catching your crib
    cards
    competitions
    & sensational scrabble
plus watching your crosswords
    (& sometimes hearing them)
for another
        5,183 days

& if you think
i'm calculating
    your perception is precise
    instincts exact
in fact
    your star-sign readouts
have you pegged

i'm calculating
    'cos i love y'.

She Knew

the woman knew
      i thought
late arrivals   guilt wiped
over me like grease on an axle
      but she didn't

she knew
      the woman knew
the woman
      selling flowers
at the market Friday night

she knew
      smiled   when i bought
two identical bunches
      smirked   the night
i started buying only one
      she knew.

Disconnected

i have pulled the plug
on our lives
    again
too many short circuits
& i'm sick of changing
fuses

two years ago
    we ran on 240 volts

but now
flat torch batteries
have more kick

go find yourself a livewire

the generator
    is seized.

Part Time Father Waiting

daily i hover over my mailbox
    making hourly vulturous swoops
in search of food

i feed   not from remains
of rotting carcass
but the beginnings
    of three young roosters
scratching out life in a northern town

they feed me & i glide
through the week
    they starve me   & i anticipate
delivery of an appointment card
    from a taxidermist.

Watching

the change in the times
is recognized differently
     by my youngest son
& my eldest

the young fellow   year three
will tell me it's 9.15 or 10.42
     his brother   year ten
tells me it's quarter past nine
     or eighteen minutes to eleven

Darth Vader digitals replace Mickey
Mouse waving his hands in playgrounds
     & clockface classwork
is dropped for basic computing skills

poor kids only have a digital watch
     rich kids
can play Space Invaders on theirs
     or lap time dad's Porsche to school

no waking to jangling bells   our digits
wake to music   or get their first
buzz for the day   controlled of course
     by their AM/FM electronic digital
bedside companion   at 6.55
     or five to seven   depending.

Drop-Ins

the unwanted have arrived
   again

it's been going on
for a week now
   seven bloody nights

bloody late nights
   & they're here
   again
uninvited   why me/why us
   we don't bloody want them

of course   they arrive
just as we slide
between the sheets
   unannouned
& for seven bloody nights
they've arrived with the
dimming of lights

not the same ones
   just the same bloody family

& we can't avoid them

we've tried
   put our heads under the pillows

but they won't leave
'till they've had a drink
   & i hate touching the stuff

but tonight
   i can't take any more
i'm out of bed padding the carpet
   & the party's on
   in our bedroom

i've bought a new label today
   & they can have the lot

as many shots as they need

& it's working
   i've found one that really works

they're falling over like
dried out drunks that've broken

& our bedroom/our bedroom
   is littered with bodies
of the intoxicated

the drop-ins
   the mosquitoes
are dying

the drop-ins
   the mosquitoes
are dead.

Bending at the Bars

Crowd Control

Terry's the bouncer
    six foot & thirteen stone

& if you're superstitious
    you could get real unlucky
with this one

he looks a cross between
a Boxer
    & a Staffordshire

& can start a blue
in an empty house (although
he'd never admit it)

in this pub
    HIS PUB
the owner
    barmen
    barmaids
    cook
& customers
    eat shit   Terry's
    & there's some big
logs amongst 'em
    'cos Terry
who used to box main events
on the east coast as
    The Blonde Bomber

is crowd control

he's known by his
train track knuckles
    steel blue eyes
    flat filleted nose
    & when his slow
deliberate drawl drones
down the bar
    don't get y'r aspirations
mixed up with y'r abilities
MUG don't

but if you reckon you've
got form he'll ask
    are you insured —
get out here on the lawn
where y' won't hit y'r head
on the way down STUPID

now i'm not religious
    but if you go —
may the good Lord
    or three of your best mates
be with you

the customer with the
compressed cheek bone
calls him   *Sir*   now
    the police   *Mister*
others   out of earshot
    call him a lunatic
others   out of hours
    call him on the phone
where they can't be reached

he deals out punishment
like a croupier
    he's not scared by
aces
    jokers
            clubs
                    or jacks

but he's got a soft spot

found it one night in a Leagues
Club in Sydney
    knocked a bloke into a coma
in 'The Eighth'

cried for 3 days —

soft they said
    bit bloody soft
oughta give the game away

& he did
    except in this pub.

26

Front Bar Closing Time

time gentlemen   time
no use yelling that in this pub
      no gentlemen
time   time   time
finish 'em up
last game on the table sport

no gentlemen in this front bar
just another 10 o'clock empty out
      tattooed truckies
plastered subbies
      tea leaves   knockabouts
& a smatter of ethnic grandfathers
(with 28″ bikes chained to the
verandah posts)

a stroll up & down the bar
      needle eyes glare
with a faint murmur of
      who's that mug
but they empty
      along with a dirty dozen
or 6 pack (cheque week or not)

& behind
      a sea of dead bingo tickets
rolls of drowned bar towel
butts ground into charcoaled
Axminster
& a million mottled glasses
      abandoned
from the top of the urinal
      to the bottom of the pool table

the last door's bolted
& blinds drawn
      money explodes from the registers

the drinking house
      turns counting house
Norman the doorman smiles
      swaggers to the lounge
ringmaster
      till midnight.

Just like Pirates Had

they reckon
    it came out as easy as a first tooth
that afternoon
    in the pub at Semaphore
& two weeks later
in the same pub
    he's half declared himself
a folk hero

reckons now
he's gunna cop it sweet
the invalid pension
    better than the dole
'cos you don't have to front
the office each week

reckons he'll kick a goal with
compo too
    heaps saw it

the other bloke just drove
two fingers straight in
    ripped it out
& stamped it
    into the front bar lino

so now
    he gets to wear
this real neat eye patch

just like pirates had.

No Trendies

just a Besser Block pub
no pretensions
    no frills
    & no bullshit

built thirty years back
by blokes with crew cuts
    square necks   & Brylcream
    smack in the guts of
the north western suburbs
    old bodgies
still drink there
    minus the Brylcream

their kids drink there too
no car salesmen
    no secretaries
    no trendies

they talk pipe dreams of
a Moomba job

take trips & speed
from a barstool

reckon rent relief's more
regular than the girlfriend
    & confuse her with
    Judy
    Debbie
    Sue
    Dianne
    Carol
tattooed down one arm
    LOVE & HATE knuckled down

& just a wrong blink
    can drive a hammer
home.

Thunderstruck

through a smoky haze
in slow-strobe
   the bouncer
thundered across the floor
& struck
       double left/right cross
& his man was down
   but not out

he clutched a handful of hair
   dragged him over polished
jarrah
    10
      20
        30 feet
& with 5 to go
   it tore away with the speed
of a champagne cork

his crown was left bald
as a baby's bum

he picked the bloke up
like a sack
   chucked him through the doorway
then bolted
      choking
with a face as white as his shirt
   with a shirt
as white as that scalp

at the stainless steel waterslide
   under the glare
of fluorescent tubes
   & others
he threw up a cup of carrots
   flicked black curls
   from his sweaty palm

grinned & announced
   i'd make a terrible hairdresser.

People in Glass Houses

it's the midnight empty
out at the pub   & i'm table
to table   packing glasses up
    & the people off

no trouble tonight she says
    & i look across to eyes
creased with a mother's concern

& tell her
people   like glasses   are fragile
should be handled with care
    some clear   some cracked
& some   with a chip on the shoulder

yet however washed up they are
    handled the right way
with allowances for flaws
    they don't   have to be destroyed.

A Carton of Beer

the blow-in could have been
an only child
    maybe   had a handful
of brothers
    but he wasn't thinking
about brotherhood in the pub
the night he tried to turn
a schooner glass into
a contact lens
    & he certainly wasn't
thinking about it when he
went back the next night
    to find twins aren't always
identical
    just close

& don't just get mad
    but even

they say the publican changed
the water in the mop bucket
3 times
    after the twin left

& now
    they're as close as a 2 day
train trip
    where one's self sentenced
to the scorch of a Nullabor camp
    a bodgie name
& working on a track
    to keep others off his

where a carton of beer
bakes in the cupboard

so it only takes one bottle
    to forget.

Bending Bars

Play The Game

swish   & the pivot-head stainless
steel razor slides off my face
like a smile
     but i can't   reflecting
on the stainless steel i felt today

razor they call it   razor wire
     looped like intestines around cold prison
walls where fire breathes from tattooed
dragons on muscled arms & eye contact
in yards is a game which costs nothing
to play but a packet of tobacco a week
     for the weak

where prison officers play kindergarten
teachers with less authority
     & the only thing they've got going
for them is
     free uniforms

where buildings get barbequed when
bargaining stops   & politicians press
the point   they can't   & won't
     negotiate with drunks

where men turn boys into men or women
     & the screams of blonde haired boys
get drowned in the maze of corridor
     where smack packs a sting
for the head & the pocket
     & the Sunday joint
means a roast if you're sprung

Yatala
     where hard labour means
200 sit ups   100 push ups   10 reps
of curls squats & bench presses

& tell that guard to fuck off
or we're going on strike
     & tell him we've scratched out
the definition of morale
from the prison dictionary
     because if we can't have it

we're not fuckin' lettin' them know
what it is.

Skin Deep

Northfield Womens' Prison
where cracks in the walls
    echo the fractured lives
of inmates

in a teenage building
    set on the same foundations
as the occupants
    The Department
patches walls

there's no underpinning
    walls or lives
the prison's cosmetic
& rehabilitation
    skin deep

the front gates sit
like massive pop-dog racks
    & open   as electric
as the atmosphere
    their impulses
run on power   others
    are cut by power

in this prison
you don't eat prunes
    movements are controlled
if you're a minute early
    you wait a minute
if you're a minute late
    you wait 29

you're taught how to be mechanical
how to cook
    clean
    sew
& knit
but you're not taught
    how to mend   or untangle

Prison lawns are manicured
    rose bushes pruned
a photographer's dream
    but inside

plaster & lives fall apart
& the women know
        even cosmetics
need foundations.

2 Weeks Later

he was unbalanced
    stood outside the front
of the chemist shop
    tottering

Louie's in doin' th' bizness
we're hangin' out man
    listen   hit the toe
we'll catch y'

his empty sleeve
flapped into his coat
pocket
    one arm   pointed
me away
    made his point
needed another

i wanted Sunblock
was scared of getting burnt
    i did

2 weeks later
    so did they.

Escapism

in a cell   8 feet x 6 feet
the prisoner writes poetry
    it's worrying the screws

where a body's locked away
    for 24 hours a day
thoughts are free for all
    thoughts   one can recall

the prisoner writes poetry
    it's worrying the screws

in a cell   8 feet x 6 feet
    for 16 hours a day
limitless thoughts are exercised
    ideals of freedom   mesmerised

the prisoner writes poetry
    it's worrying the screws

in a cell   8 feet x 6 feet
the prisoner builds a library
    cuts through pages   sharp-eyed
hacks out evidence   of owners

the prisoner   reads poetry
    it's worrying the screws

then recites it
    explores it   abhors it
re-lives it   escapes it
    applauds it

the prisoner writes poetry
    & it's worrying the screws.

Full of Pricks

after the prisoners tended cactus garden within an exercise yard at
Yatala Labour Prison

A burst of bell
    & eyes focus
through mirror glass

the prison door's
heaved back with
British authority
    yes   bites at me
with 6 o'clock chill

er   poetry workshop
    & he throws a look
behind me to see if i've
left a beard outside

the English guard
directs me to a British
man who sends me
to a U.K. chap
    & while i sign
his book
    the British man
searches my bag

i'm given a green clip card
    number 21
& a clearance

assigned to a Yorkshire
bloke
    & marshalled through
an exercise yard
to "B" Division

i open my mouth
& fall out of step between
verbal & metal grills
    when i'm handed over
to a Lancashire lad
    who points/grunts
poetry workshop   upstairs

2 flights of metal treads
    6 sets of steel eyes
& the warm English welcome
chills me
    it's in there   coldest
room in the place   poetry eh
    what would they know
about bloody poetry

i pace the concrete floor
    70 by 30
9 tables   24 chairs
6 ashtrays   & wait
    while 3 guards have
their schoolboy giggle
on the landing

then a voice crackles
through speakers
like a football commentator
    there is a poetry
workshop commencing now
in G Top for all prisoners

& over the balustrade
swings a Londoner
    reciting in royal blue
the boy stood on the
burnin' deck

& i'm left cold   thinking
    poetry eh   well you've
just shown me what you know —
    & guards' laughter
rings reality up the stairwell

i stop pacing
    undo my green card
& bite its alligator teeth
to my tongue
    think about prejudice
oppression
    power   restraint

& wonder if that cactus
garden in the exercise yard

stands as a symbol
    of passive protest.

(No) Smoking In The Education Centre

fourteen men shuffle
through hospital-wide corridors
    for a poetry performance
at Port Lincoln Prison

an officer stands at full forward
    booms at a prisoner
put that cigarette out
    y' know there's no smoking
allowed between buildings
    yes   the thing in y'r hand
get it out

the red bit goes in an ashtray
    goalpost in the pocket —
the officer boots home his point
    & there's no awards
for best & fairest

we're bundled into the education
centre where a sign reads
    NO SMOKING
but ask any prisoner & you'll
be told — *rules are made to be ...*

i light up a cigar
    read to intent eyes
over the rustle of Tally Ho
& plastic pouches
    prison poems
pub poems
    junkie poems
people poems
    kick out leads
they can score off
& see positions adopted
all around the room

nearby in the corridor
    the senior officer
chats to their tutor
    but he's so far removed
he could be in a P.O.W. camp
    his English brogue leads
off with

look at 'im with 'is cigar
poets should 'ave a cigarette
in a long thin 'older

after an hour & a half
        fourteen men have been moved —
then moved again

they're taken back
        & the tutor & i wonder —
just how far

we leave
        talking of cigarettes & cigars
poetry & prison readings
& whether all officers link poets
        with cigarettes
cigars
        or just fags.

Locked Out

Like A Cross-Word Puzzle

it was 8.40 a.m.
a major arterial road
    nearly everyone
in a hurry

i caught sight of him
moving to the edge
of the footpath
    Aboriginal
shorts T-shirt
& airways bag

he dropped it
    adopted that stance —
left foot well forward
    raised his right hand
faced the oncoming traffic
& fired
      bang-bang bang-bang
bang-bang from
what i thought could be
a .45 calibre revolver

i veered to the left

he'd missed me

i caught sight of him
    blowing smoke
from his fingertips
    smiling
through teeth spaced
like a cross-word puzzle

his big sister   around
eleven
    spun her head 90°
then 180°
yelled
    Michael   everyone's
watchin'   hurry up or we'll
be late for school

he just stood in the gutter
wondering

lessons for Michael
    were just beginning.

Moved On

*after the positioning of a flower bed in an area of lawn fronting the
Hilton Hotel, Victoria Square, Adelaide previously occupied by
Aboriginals for socialising.*

sundrenched flowers
stand
   where people sat
a staggered circle
in the square
   looking up
to doors that open
   closed to them

squeezing juice
from necks of flagons
losing life
   short bursts of mouth
to mouth   resuscitate
a courage lost
   & drown their dream

while politicians pass
in office hours
   feed promises
of crusty loaves
& deliver goods
   as empty as their words

the sun is gone
   & wilted stalks
& drooping heads remain
   while others search
for beds
   & International lights
that shape the square
wink down

they've moved the circle on.

Bitter This — Bitter That

There was a handy doctor
in the days of prohibition

opted —
for the hypocritic oath

butchered under 60 watts
in a Blair Athol bedroom

then dug in buckets of the stuff
around the lemon tree

none of his mates could bear
to take a boxfull home

beauties that they were —
big as babies' heads.

Right on — Right off

they'd arrested my attention
       guiding this raspy-voiced blackfella
out of the Central Market Mall

just waltzing along
       blue uniform either side

all travelling
       no touching
just talking

& then

they detour through the fish market
to the stalls
       (which were closed)

i'm out into Gouger Street
       drop into Marinos Meat
for the mince
(it's spaghetti night)
       & back to the street

the dog box is out front

i'm a bit surprised
they haven't lobbed

think about the options —

decide to walk back
       when i'm locked to the bitumen

Bubbleguts at about 14 stone
is trying to break the
bloke's right arm

Slim   with messy blonde hair
that's just fallen out of its cap
is going to town on the left

struggling to save
the bottle of Southwark
that's still capped

they're down the kerb
to the back of the box

a handful of hair

& the blackfella's forehead
sounds like a bass drum
on the door ledge

he's off nighty-nights

they catch him before
he hits the deck
   up him like a chaff bag
& belly-flop him to the floor

a little Italian hairdresser
taking a short black
in the coffee shop
   comes out   watches   as legs
are twisted back to seal a blokes chances

i've yelled
   do y' do that to everyone
or just blackfellas y' bastards

shaddup or you'll be off too

off i says   *you're off*
right fuckin' off
   UGB 510   3.29 p.m.
we'll see who's off

& he is —
   to the watch-house

i've asked the little bloke
to back me on a statement
   Noo sorri   police make too
mush trubel for me
   lika to elp but carn tak charnce
yoo unnerstan

i leave him with
next time it might be your brother —
   or you

later ...
   i front the Duty Inspector
make a statement —

any other witnesses
i tell him about the hairdresser
   & the other Aboriginal
the one walking home after work

51

how they were both scared of
getting involved
    police intimidation & all that

& 6 weeks later

no-one's been in touch
    no follow up
so i guess i know now

who's off

or what's off.

Illegal Entry

Monday morning
a city house
    & two men enter
to the slap
of a flyscreen door

four squatters
have become fifteen
    overnight
all wear schoolboy smiles
    & their wardrobes

one of the men
flips back the door
like the lid of a coffin
    while a squatter grins
turns on a tape recorder
    takes out a camera

OUT
    the command
is as short
as the man's temper
OUT

fifteen squatters
    separated from the footpath
by fifteen feet
are now airborne
    & in fifteen seconds
fifteen bodies
    are mounded outside

one scrambles
from under the pile
    snaps photographs
& abuse
at the blind and deaf
    while his tape
absorbs drama
    like a sponge

the talkative man
stands in the doorway
like a bulldog
    snarls *DON'T*

53

& points a thick
calloused finger
at the gate

the other
    hurls blankets, pots,
pans, plates, vegemite,
stale bread rolls
& a bong
    onto bitumen
while squatters spit venom
at porcelain eyes

the owner arrives
in a chocolate BMW
    his truck follows
laden with heavy timber
    & five heavy carpenters
to brace windows & doors

in two hours
    the blind & the deaf
are paid
    all remnants of occupation
are gone
    & the house
is as protected
    as its owner

tonight
    through necessity
fifteen kids
    will rape another house.

On Meeting a Radio Announcer

You had to be tuned in
at the right time
 to catch his words

faceless words
 flying over airwaves
bounced from black boxes
& strained through mesh

but facing the words un-strained
 they slide with laminex gloss
over a kitchen table & Turkish coffee
 while we talk
multi-cultural Australia

he's announced
i've never met an intelligent black

& a Greek lady says
 you're a racist

he disagrees looks for support —
 no y'r not a racist
y'r definitely not a racist
 & his dial changes its appearance

y'r a bigot

& he turns his volume down

the static
 has affected his ratings.

Insulated

10 years ago
    he exchanged his cash
for a flawless blue
solitaire diamond
    for her

at the hock shop today
    she swapped it
for 3 months electricity
    2 months gas
    6 weeks rent
& an hour
    in the supermarket

the sparkle's left her eyes
as she shuffles away
on rubber thongs that give
no insulation
    the spark was fused
long ago   ignited
    on the burps & farts
of 8 years booze
    the gas went long before
today's final notice

as she eases herself
into her car
    a lawnmower's mouth
gapes from the boot
    she's cut down to the sharpness
of grit under foot

the pawnbroker
flashes a golden smile
    he's wearing someone else's
wet-suit
    he's fully insulated.

To Remember

sixteen years young
midsummer
    bumfluff & pimples
i worked with Brian

asked
    what happened to y'r face?

he talked about a marriage bust
    kids caught in a revolving door
& nights strapped down in the
nutcracker suite
    of how he grew to hate himself

one night
    at the mirror ...
shaving ...

... sixteen years later
    i wonder
if i could hate myself enough
midsummer
    & shave off a beard
to remember.

On To Andamooka

the bitumen river
shimmers with deceit
   water's only a memory
white lines   road signs   calcified bones
& dead echoes

Australia's bonsai gardens   broken
by graveyards
cattle grids & railway track

sheep   magnetized to a dry trough
& mauve becomes red
   upstream
past shifting sandhills   more travelled
than Bullens Circus
   & on through saltpans
bordered by glaring quartz
tired rubber   intolerant mufflers
& scattered rusting carcasses
screamed to rest

monuments of grief decay
slowly to the fade of faces

into Pimba where nothing's wasted

& on to Andamooka.

The Waiting Room

no more work   the doctor said
no more
no more booze   *you'll lose*   he said
no more

no more   *dat's bullshit half dat talk*
no more

no more no less   it's all the same
no more
no more goons   for breakfast Lou
no more
no more medicine   at the local Lou
no more
no more trips   to the doctor Lou
no more
no more colour   for Claxton Street
no more
no more Lou   no more
no more.

Caged

at 38   his youth's tattooed
over him like a roadmap
     & the eagle on his chest
has its claws dug in hard
     on her

there's no flying away
     wings clipped by two kids
& the worry of that .38
in the top drawer

all i can do is hug the kids
in tight when he gets home
she sobs   *I don't think*
he'd belt THEM

& it's dewdrops on the nostrils
hayfever eyes for all seasons
     there's no new horizons
& no place   far enough away

she's caged to a life of
asprins & empties —
watches late night tattooes
     sees H A T E
blueprinted
     into both claws.

What Chance Has A Bloke Got

listen he says
you've heard i've lost me cook
haven't y'

yeah   i've heard
a bit of a whisper

well   can i buy y' one
& get in y'r ear
she's got me stumped
    dead set

he's backed me into a corner
& said   *25 bloody years*
& she lobs this on me
    no other bloke
just this bloody womens'
liberation bullshit
    wants to be on her own

i've told her
    if there's a mug   you're off
& if i know him   he's off too
    but no   no mug   just muggins me
i mean look at me
    five foot nothing
a fat ex-jockey who can skin rabbits
& rock'n'roll
    what chance has a bloke got

she's moved into a flat
on her pat malone
    left me on the farm with
me 2 lads   the horses
& the dogs

i've worked me guts out
all me life
    2 jobs plus breaking horses
on the weekends
    even chucked a leg
over a few windowsills
when things got really desperate
    she's never had to ask f'r
a thing   not a bloody thing

told her to get home f'r
lunch Mother's Day
    & she come too —
we're in the kitchen
by the back door
& i says to her
    y' see that Palomino colt
out there
    she says 'yeah'
& i said   that's mine

& i says y' see that
blue heeler pup over there
    she says 'yeah'
& i said   that's mine

& i says now get over there
& look in that bloody mirror
'cos that's mine too
    you're going nowhere

& she's up & hoofed it
    women   y' just can't work
'em out   i've given her everything
    given her the bloody lot

yeah   i said   you sure have.

Biographical Note

Geoff Goodfellow was born in Adelaide in 1949. Started writing late in 1982 when a severe back injury forced an early retirement from the building industry. During 1984 he became active in Schools, Colleges and Institutions with performance readings, discussions and workshops. These have been held within TAFE Colleges, State and Private Schools, Aboriginal Education groups, E.P.U.Y. Centres, Gaols and Reformatories. Together with Jenny Boult and Eric Beach (with assistance from the S.A. Department For the Arts) he was a member of the "New Mobile Poetry Workshop" during 1984/85 which encouraged the writing of contemporary Australian poetry. He was Secretary of the S.A. Poets Union in 1984. Performed a guest reading at Friendly Street in October, 1984 and is a regular reader at the Cathedral Hotel and other Adelaide venues. Attended Montsalvat in 1984 and combined this visit to include readings at Pentridge Gaol and the Lienster Arms Hotel. During 1985 he read at the Festival Centre Gallery "Spark Sessions", Tasmanian Poetry Festival, Hobart Writers' Union, Footscray Institute of Technology and was appointed Poet In Residence at Pembroke School, Yatala Labour Prison and SAYRAC and SAYTC Reformatories. Yatala Labour Prison has again engaged his services for 1986 and both reformatories have re-appointed him for 1986 — through the Schools Commission Funding for Children in Residential Care. He recently edited *Lifting the Weight*, an anthology of childrens poetry written through his 1985 residency. He is a part-time father of three boys and lives within the square mile of Adelaide.